PIANO / VOCAL / GUITAR

ADELE 21

ISBN 978-1-4584-0223-3

HAL•LEONARD®
CORPORATION

7777 W. BLUEMOUND RD. P.O. BOX 13819 MILWAUKEE, WI 53213

Visit Hal Leonard Online at
www.halleonard.com

ROLLING IN THE DEEP

Words and Music by ADELE ADKINS
and PAUL EPWORTH

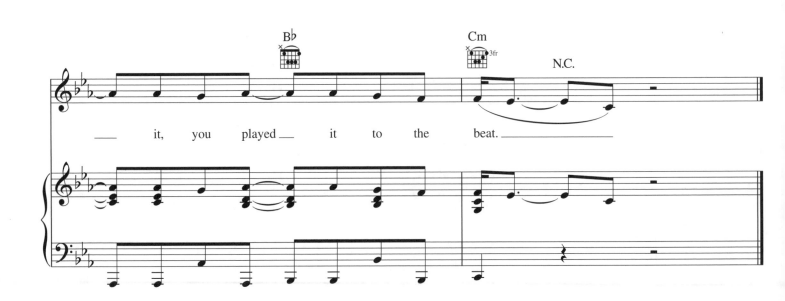

RUMOUR HAS IT

Words and Music by ADELE ADKINS
and RYAN TEDDER

With energy and soul

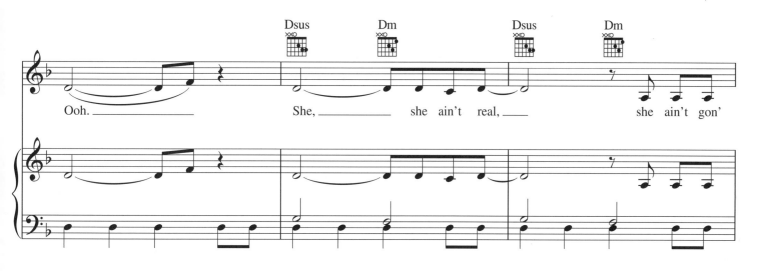

TURNING TABLES

Words and Music by ADELE ADKINS
and RYAN TEDDER

DON'T YOU REMEMBER

Words and Music by ADELE ADKINS
and DAN WILSON

Slow acoustic Ballad

When will I see you _____ a - gain? _____ You left with
When was the last time you thought of me? _____ Or have you

no good- bye, not a sin - gle word _____ was said. _____ No
com - plete- ly e - rased me from your mem - o - ry? _____ I of - ten

the rea - son you loved me _____ be -

- fore? Ba - by, please re - mem - ber me once ___

more. When will I see you ___ a - gain? _____

SET FIRE TO THE RAIN

Words and Music by ADELE ADKINS
and FRASER SMITH

HE WON'T GO

Words and Music by ADELE ADKINS
and PAUL EPWORTH

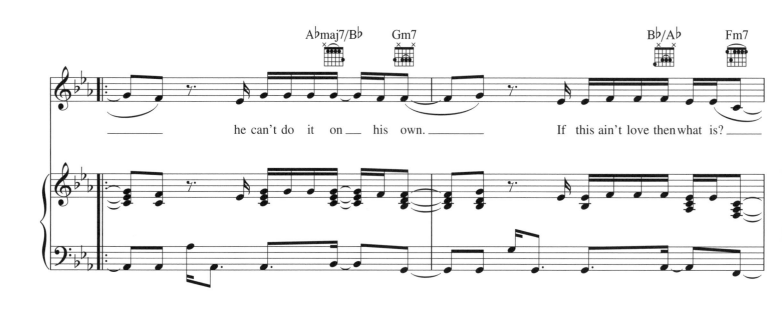

TAKE IT ALL

Words and Music by ADELE ADKINS
and FRANCIS EG WHITE

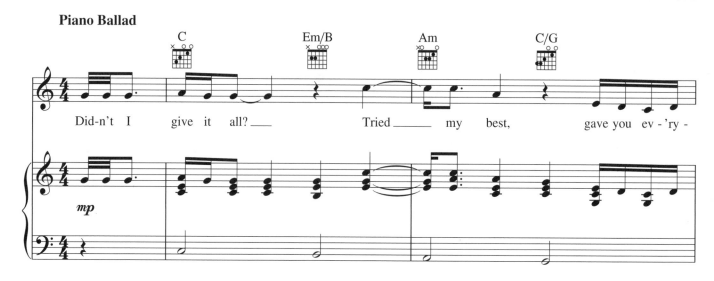

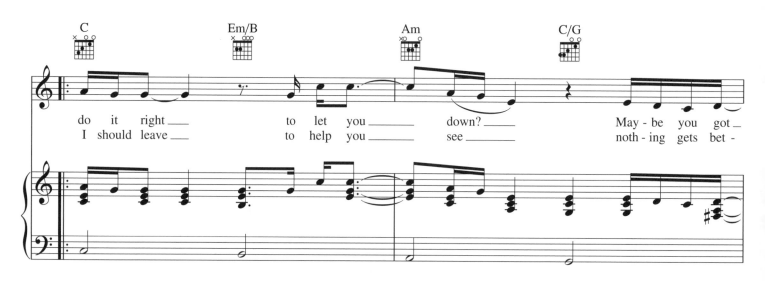

I'LL BE WAITING

Words and Music by ADELE ADKINS
and PAUL EPWORTH

54

ONE AND ONLY

Words and Music by ADELE ATKINS,
DAN WILSON and GREG WELLS

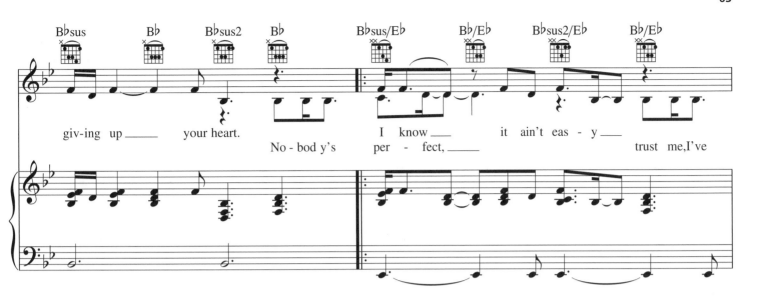

giv-ing up _____ your heart.
No - bod y's per - fect, _____ it ain't eas - y _____ trust me, I've

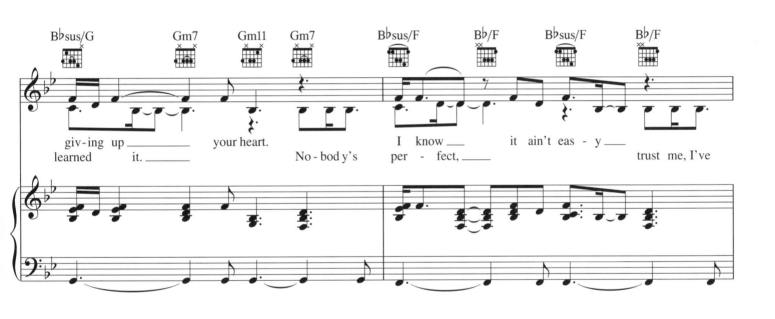

giv-ing up _____ your heart.
learned it. _____ No - bod y's per - fect, _____ it ain't eas - y _____ trust me, I've

giv-ing up _____ your heart.
learned it. _____ No - bod-y's

giv-ing up _____ your
learned it. _____

starts. _____ Come on _____ and give me a chance _ to prove I am the

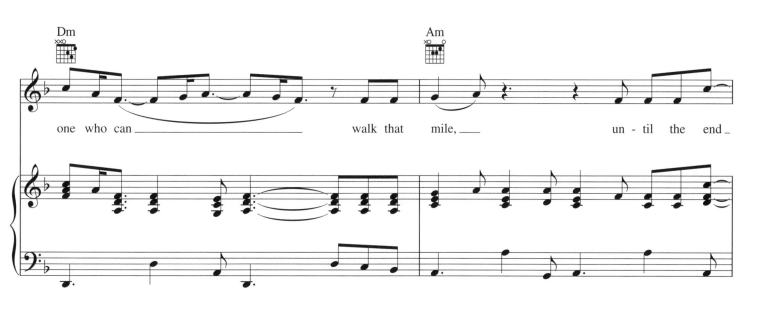

one who can _____ walk that mile, ___ un-til the end _

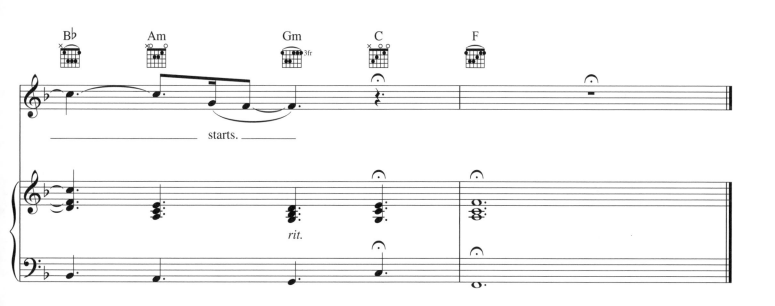

starts. _____

LOVESONG

Words and Music by ROBERT SMITH,
LAURENCE TOLHURST, SIMON GALLUP,
PAUL S. THOMPSON, BORIS WILLIAMS
and ROGER O'DONNELL

Slow groove

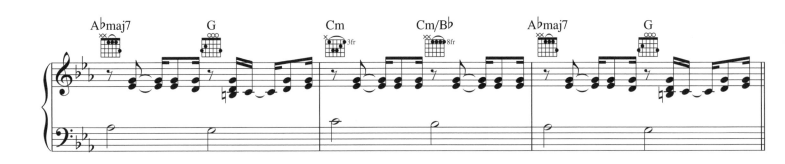

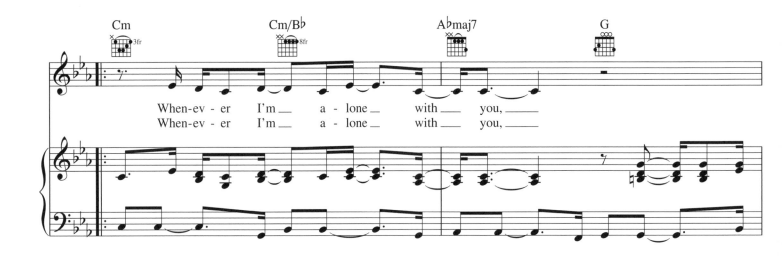

When-ev - er I'm __ a - lone __ with __ you, _____
When-ev - er I'm __ a - lone __ with __ you, _____

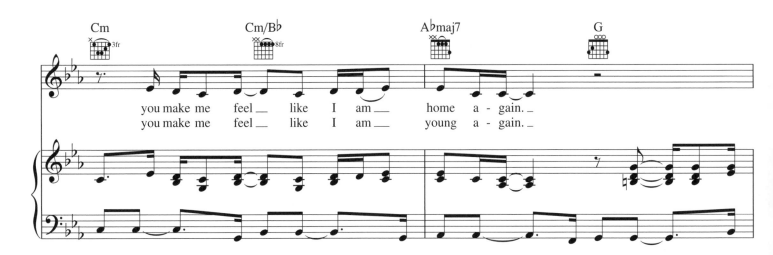

you make me feel __ like I am __ home a - gain. __
you make me feel __ like I am __ young a - gain. __

ev - er I'm a - lone ____ with ____ you, ____

D.S. al Coda

you make me feel ____ like I am ____ clean a - gain. ____

CODA

I will al - ways love ____ you. ____

Vocal tacet on repeat

Guitar solo

you,   I'll al - ways ____ love you. ____   I'll al - ways ____

____ love you. ____   'Cause I love ___ you. ____

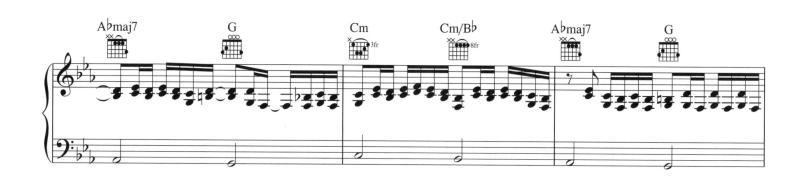

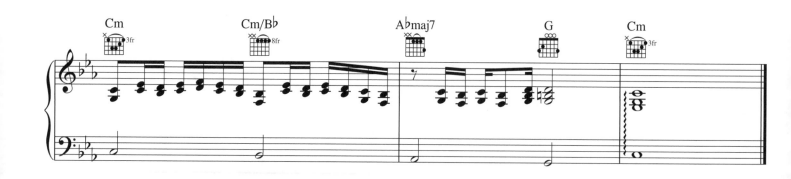

SOMEONE LIKE YOU

Words and Music by ADELE ADKINS
and DAN WILSON